FAMILIUS

Copyright © 2017 by Linda Perret and Gene Perret
Illustrations copyright © 2017 by Adam Eastburn

Published by Familius LLC, www.familius.com

Familius books are available at special discounts for bulk purchases, whether
for sales promotions or for family or corporate use. For more information,
contact Familius Sales at 559-876-2170 or email orders@familius.com.

Library of Congress Cataloging-in-Publication Data

2016961591

ISBN 9781944822873

Printed in China

Edited by DeAnna Acker

Cover design by David Miles

Book design by Adam Eastburn

10 9 8 7 6 5 4 3 2 1

First Edition

Being pregnant is like having company for nine months.

And 174 Other Laughs (Because you'll need them) for the

Mom-to-be

by GENE PERRET & LINDA PERRET with
Illustrations by Adam Eastburn

Mom-to-be, you're starting out on a new journey —
an adventure called motherhood.
And it is going to be wonderful.

Oh, sure, there may be some rough spots. You may have some moments of discomfort, have a few doubts, and face many changes. That sexy figure you spent years in the gym to achieve is going to disappear almost overnight, along with your feet. You will develop cravings for food that you never knew existed and will indulge them at hours of the night that you never wanted to know existed.

But if becoming a mom was easy, your husband would have volunteered to do it. And if men were responsible for the miracle of childbirth, babies would be whittled out of wood or would be electronic gadgets you had to plug in.

No, ladies, this little event is all yours. The men just get to watch from the sidelines. And lucky for you, because the whole experience is magnificent. After all, you get to know your little one before anyone else. So while you're expecting, enjoy it, relish it, and maybe even milk it a little bit.

With a sense of humor and lots of love, you have everything you need to tackle every moment of your pregnancy and all the years of being "mom."

—Linda Perret and Gene Perret

I must be pregnant.
I have cravings for pickles, for ice
cream, and to bite someone's head
off for no good reason.

I'm pregnant.
Ask if you can have one of my
french fries at your own risk.

What they teach in law school is excellent advice: never ask a woman if she's pregnant unless you absolutely know the answer.

Think before you speak to a pregnant woman. Hormonal imbalance is a recognized legal defense for mayhem.

Be wary of what you say to a pregnant woman. If they can bring life into the world, they can sure as heck knock the life out of you.

Moms know everything,
and the amazing thing is that they
learned it all in 9 months.

If men had babies, the words *sister* and *brother* would have become obsolete long ago.

You can't rush a pregnancy. In fact,
when you're pregnant, you can't even
rush getting in and out of a car.

Remember the nursery rhyme "Jack be nimble, Jack be quick"?

He wouldn't have been either if he were 7 months pregnant.

It's often said that
"it takes two to tango."
In the later stages of pregnancy, it
often takes two to get up from
a sitting position.

After being pregnant for a few months, one begins to realize that the kangaroo was onto something with that pouch idea.

It's a good thing that the fetus
isn't like regular children. All during
the pregnancy it would demand
a seat by a window.

How inconvenient being pregnant
can sometimes be. It's like having
company stay for 9 months.

As a pregnant woman, I discovered that when I lay down in bed, I could no longer see the television.

It's strange to hear a woman say, "My biological clock was ticking." It sounds like they have a wind-up uterus.

Once you discover that you're pregnant, you're going to have to resign yourself to the fact that you're probably not going to win many more limbo contests.

I grow larger every day.
I feel like the national debt.

All pregnant women must
realize there's no such thing as
a maternity bikini.

Though I'm pregnant,
I still have a compact figure.
I look like a Volkswagen.

If I'm so uncomfortable, how come the baby in the ultrasound images looks so relaxed?

One duty of a pregnant woman is pretending that you can actually see something in those ultrasound images.

Sitting down when you're pregnant can be difficult because you realize that, at some point, you're going to have to get up again.

While you're pregnant, you have all
kinds of weird cravings:

potato chips, pizza, getting up out a
chair without help.

Pregnancy can get a bit demoralizing when even your bathrobes have to be let out.

Ankles sometimes swell during pregnancy. Why should they be any different from the rest of your body?

Pregnancy can be trying for 9 long months, but you're rewarded with a trophy you will love forever.

During pregnancy, your body goes through some drastic changes, and some of them are pretty scary.

Like when you open your mouth and your mother's voice comes out.

Pregnancy is the 9 months of
parenthood leading up to when
the real work begins.

Soon you'll have a beautiful child who will love, honor, and obey you . . . at least until the teenage years.

Spend lots of time deciding on a name for your baby. You want a first and a middle name that has meaning, is stylish, and easily rolls off the tongue when you're angry.

Pregnant women should realize
that they have restricted
mobility. They should not make
any sudden, strenuous movements
unless food is involved.

I have food cravings all the time.
Being pregnant just provides me a
convenient excuse.

One delicate question is: when should pregnant women have sex?

Well, certainly before.

You realize no matter where you go when you're pregnant, you're always second in line.

The child in the womb should be grateful. This may be the last time it has its own room.

The baby must feel cramped inside the womb . . . but then, it's good training for the dorm room it's going to have in college.

There are definitely some perks to being a mom. From now on, you are going to be on the receiving end of all those Mother's Day brunches.

The first thing babies do when
they're born is cry. If they could talk,
the first thing they would say is, "Boy,
it feels good to stretch my legs."

All pregnanies involve a man, a woman, and a baby. Of the three, the baby is probably the only one who really knows exactly what he's doing.

I can't believe that my husband helped me make a baby. He normally doesn't even help when I'm making sandwiches.

In a few short months, you'll
have a little baby around the house
to take care of . . . other than
the one you married.

If pregnancy were all fun and games,
men would have created a fantasy
league to go along with it.

If pregnancy were a book, men would
be only the dedication page.

It's interesting how Mother Nature handles procreation. It seems that immediately after conception, the male says to the female, "OK, you can take it from here."

I think I'll let my husband have the next baby. Let me hand out the cigars for a change.

My husband and I were thrilled when the pregnancy test showed positive. It's the first test either one of us has passed since the eighth grade.

Women have the children because they endure pain better than men do. Pain to a man is when he's sitting on the couch watching a football game with a beer in one hand and snack food in the other and the team he's rooting for fumbles.

It's ironic that my husband and
I built an entirely new person
together. Normally we avoid buying
anything that says

"SOME ASSEMBLY REQUIRED."

One thought runs through the mind
of every father-to-be at some time
during his mate's pregnancy:

Boy, did I luck out being born a man.

Everything swells when you're pregnant—including your husband's head.

It's only fair. Since men neither get pregnant nor give birth, they should be satisfied with less closet space.

With some women, as the belly gets larger, the temper gets shorter.

My husband likes to talk to the baby
in my womb. Why? Because lately,
he's afraid to talk to me.

My husband and I had some terrible spats while I was pregnant, but I always won. I had him outnumbered.

Try playing learning tapes to the child in the womb. Imagine how proud you'll be when your baby's first words are in French.

If you read to your child while in the womb, the fetus will immediately develop a love of books. It may take a little longer to learn to turn the pages.

House hunting is common among expectant parents. When you're pregnant, you feel as though you need more room. They baby has the same feeling.

One thought runs through every
woman's mind while she's expecting:

*Only a man could have
invented pregnancy.*

Soon you'll be a mother — the highest
ranking in the civilian world.

. . . In any world, for that matter.

Carrying a new life is a miraculous and joyous experience. Couldn't they have come up with a better-sounding word than "pregnant"?

The doctor told me I'd be eating for two now. I was too embarrassed to tell him that I was doing that before the pregnancy.

Yes, pregnancy can be pure
awkwardness and frustration, but then
it produces pure love.

Being a new mom is educational.
You're finally going to know the true
meaning of the phrase "at wit's end."

Another good thing about
pregnancy — it doesn't last nearly as
long as the presidential campaigns.

I read a book about pregnancy once.
It took me 9 months to finish it.

When you are pregnant, read as many expert books on mothering as you can. That way, when you make a mistake, you have plenty of people to blame.

They say that pregnant women
seem to glow. That's because
their skin stretches so much
it becomes translucent.

Sure, they describe a pregnant woman as "glowing." That sounds so much nicer than "fat and grouchy."

My mother said something to me
while we were shopping for maternity
clothes. She said, "Don't worry,
honey. You'll grow into them."

If you have butterflies in your stomach, that means you're nervous. If one of them starts kicking you, that means you're pregnant.

It's hard to get a goodnight's sleep with a child using your insides as a trampoline.

This is my first pregnancy. I ordered
8x10s of the ultrasound image
for the entire family.

Being pregnant is when you first realize that the term "fashionable maternity clothes" is an oxymoron.

Pregnancy means never having to say,
"Do you have this in a smaller size?"

Pregnancy is educational. I now know how to spell "trimester."

Pregnancy is when someone says,
"Your shoes are really cute," and
you have to say, "I forget. Tell me
what they look like."

During your pregnancy, you may
experience some new and strange
cravings—like the desire to
see your feet again.

Pregnancy is 9 months. But I bet
you'd be willing to settle for 6 months
and some community service.

Elephants are pregnant for about 22 months. But then on the bright side, they don't have to shop for maternity clothes.

Pregnancy for white mice is about 19 days, which is why white mice rarely have baby showers. There's just not enough time to plan for it.

It's easy for a pregnant woman to get a seat on a crowded bus. It's not so easy to get out of it again.

Pregnancy is approximately 9
months of answering the question,
"How do you feel?"

If you think being pregnant is tough, consider this: it may be the easiest part of parenthood.

In birthing class, they teach you all kinds of breathing exercises to help manage the pain. Pay close attention; they will come in handy during both the delivery and the teen years.

Pregnancy means never having to say, "You dropped something. Here, I'll pick it up for you."

I'm pregnant. Both of my grandparents can now beat me in a "get out of the chair fastest" contest.

If you want to know what it feels like to be pregnant, try driving from the backseat of your car.

The closest thing to being pregnant
is the person who carries the big bass
drum in the school marching band.

Pregnancy is like pushing a loaded wheelbarrow for 9 months . . . with the front wheel missing.

One good thing about being
pregnant—your breasts get
bigger for free.

If you think pregnancy is an ordeal,
wait till the kid arrives.

Pregnancy lasts 9 months. It takes that long to build up to the joy of having a baby.

When people ask if I'm pregnant,
I say, "Have you ever seen anything this
size that wasn't?"

Pregnancy produces some strange sensations. For instance, I always feel like I'm hiding behind something.

People ask, "Are you showing?"
In photographs, I look surprisingly like
Half Dome Mountain.

Lately, travel has become difficult.
Which is ironic, since I'm the
size of a Winnebago.

Pregnancy may be uncomfortable for you at times, but consider this: it may be the greatest time the baby has ever had.

I seem to grow larger every day. I'm now larger than the room I lived in during my college days.

I used to have a very athletic body,
and now I'm pregnant. But I still look
like an athlete: a sumo wrestler.

Avoid asking an expectant mother,
"When do you figure the baby is due?"

(NEVER say the word "figure" to a
pregnant woman.)

I knew when I got pregnant I would
lose my girlish figure, but I didn't know
my feet would disappear.

Before I became pregnant, I ate like a bird. Now I eat like a wood chipper.

How come if I'm eating for two, only one of us gets morning sickness?

"Morning sickness" is an unpleasant term. But it is preferred to "barfing before noon."

Whenever you feel weary about being pregnant, think about chickens. Isn't this process better than sitting on an egg for 9 months?

Being pregnant means never having to say, "Lets go bowling tonight."

Here's a warning to women who have
just discovered they're pregnant —
Pilates class is going to get tougher.

Pregnancy can sometimes be trying, but remember: all of the problems will be gone in approximately 9 months and 38 years.

The whole process of creating a new life is a miracle. It's one of the few miracles that will later have to be sent to college.

I shouldn't complain about being pregnant. I love children. But they're easier to deal with when they're on the outside of your body.

One good thing about being
pregnant — you're at least 24 months
away from "the terrible twos."

When you're pregnant, everywhere you go, you have a passenger. It's like 9 months of being an Uber driver.

Once a woman discovers she's
pregnant, it's comforting to know
that for the next 9 months, she
will never be alone.

. . . And neither will the baby.

If husbands and wives alternated having children, the overpopulation situation would solve itself.

The doctor gave my husband a book on pregnancy, and he's doing well with it. He's got almost all of the pages colored.

Having a new baby is nature's way of
saying, "You've slept enough."

Avoid the term "bun in the oven."
When you're ready to deliver, you want
to be taken to a hospital, not a bakery.

Husbands especially don't like the term "a bun in the oven." They consider themselves lovers, not bakers.

They say when you are pregnant, you have a bun in the oven. Pretty soon you'll discover the baker may have used a little too much yeast.

Why are people so eager to know the sex of the baby? It shouldn't really matter to them. It surely won't matter to the baby for a while.

To guarantee that your child will
have cute sports-inspired attire, you
should get an ultrasound that not only
predicts that baby's gender but also
its favorite sports teams.

A practical gift for a woman who is pregnant is a map of every restroom in the continental United States.

Love means never having to say you're sorry. Pregnancy means always having to say, "Where's the ladies' room?"

Pregnancy is basically 9 months
of discomfort interrupted by 1 day
for the baby shower.

There are many uncomfortable moments during a pregnancy, not the least of which is the baby shower.

A baby shower is where you get a
bunch of things you want along with a
bunch of advice you don't.

If you want to make money from your pregnancy, have someone give you a quarter for every time you hear the phrase "Isn't that darling?" at the baby shower.

One thing about baby showers—
it's usually easy to see who the
guest of honor is.

A baby shower is an excuse to buy
cute clothing that no child who has
reached the age of reason would wear.

At the baby shower, you'll get
enough baby clothes to last
until the kid is 16.

Pregnancy makes a woman more empathetic. When I see a man with a beer belly now, I can understand what he's going through.

When you're pregnant, everybody wants to rub your belly. Now I have an idea how Buddha feels.

When people ask if they can feel my belly, I say, "Yes; can I bite your nails?"

When I was pregnant, so many people
rubbed my belly that when I gave birth,
I thought a genie was going to pop out.

The reason pregnancy lasts only
9 months is because by the end of 9
months you're about sick of all the
advice you've gotten from friends.

When it comes to all the wonderful advice you'll get while pregnant, there's really only one thing you need to know—don't listen.

Take all the advice and old wives'
tales that friends offer, multiply
them by two, and you still only
have half-truths.

It's amazing how many old wives' tales you'll hear while you're pregnant. Even more amazing is just how many old wives there are out there.

If women offer advice about your pregnancy, tactfully ignore it. If men give you advice, punch them.

Pregnant women learn to develop new strategies for the third trimester. For instance, they learn to drop only things that they won't have to pick up for at least 3 months.

Things get serious during the
third trimester. You're running out
of time to try to pretend to enjoy
Dr. Seuss books.

During the last few months of pregnancy, learn a few pleasant lullabies. If you're a good singer, they may lull the child to sleep. If you're a bad singer, the baby may just pretend to sleep so you'll stop singing.

Nesting is the part of your
pregnancy where the baby says,
"Ready or not, here I come."

In about the seventh month of your pregnancy, don't you wish you still believed that the stork brought the babies?

Some people say a stork brings a new baby. I think they are lying, and I have the stretch marks to prove it.

Pregnancy lasts 8 months
and 1 eternity.

The first trimester is 3 months long. The second trimester is 3 months long. The third trimester is whatever the baby wants it to be.

Women can sometimes become irritable toward the end of their pregnancy. In fact, it could be that maternity leave is actually for the benefit of the *other* people at work.

My doctor said I should avoid anything strenuous. I wonder what he considers giving birth?

When I was impatient with my pregnancy, my Grandmom used to say, "When the apple is ripe, it will fall." I said, "Grandmom, if I go through all this and have an apple, I'm going to be teed off."

My husband's mother keeps saying the same thing: "When the apple is ripe, it will fall." Great, I not only have to put up with morning sickness but also a mother-in-law who thinks I'm a tree.

A baby will be born when it's
ready . . . which is usually about 2
months after you are.

There's a reason why pregnancy lasts
9 months. That's how long it takes a
mom to develop her superpowers.

At the end of 9 months, I wasn't
ready to deliver. So I had my
accountant file an extension.

The hospital we went to wouldn't
permit videotaping of the actual birth,
so we hired a courtroom artist.

For 7 months after I gave birth,
anytime I came to a door that said
"Push," I punched it.

I'm going to miss being pregnant.
I kind of got used to my feet
being in the shade.

When the pregnancy is over, the only one in your house who will sleep like a baby is the baby.

While you are expecting, you'll get
all kinds of strange cravings. After
the baby comes, there's only one thing
you'll crave . . . sleep.

Experienced parents will tell
you that the best name for the
new baby is "Insomnia."

All your baby wants is nourishment,
protection, and love. It won't be
that long, though, until she also
wants a tattoo.

It's fun to watch them grow,
learn, and mature. Not the baby —
the husband.

Mothers-to-be should be aware
that when the baby comes home, the
other children may be jealous . . . and
that includes the husband.

Pregnant women produce a baby
just like a magician pulling a rabbit out
of a hat. Except it doesn't take the
magician 9 months, and he doesn't have
to send the rabbit to college.

As a new mom, dressing for success means wearing anything that doesn't have spit-up on it.

Once the child arrives,
the spit-up rag becomes your
new fashion accessory.

Being a new mom is 9 months of being pregnant followed by at least 9 months of people telling you who the baby looks like.

Everyone who visits my house wants
to hold the new baby. Where were all
these people when I was carrying?

When you bring your new baby home, you'll get lots of visitors and they'll all want to hold the baby. The parents should hand them the baby then go out for a nice, quiet dinner.

If you want to have some fun as a new mother, ask visitors not to talk baby talk to your child. After about 20 minutes, the visitors will have a nervous breakdown.

It seems that everyone who visits wants to hold the new baby. What you should do is take names and then call them when the kid wakes up at 2:00 in the morning.

Face it. For the next couple of years, diapers will be an important part of your life.

Pick out a nice, extra-large, super-cumbersome baby bag. Let the man carry something heavy around for the next 9 months.

The second pregnancy is always easier. If you drop something on the floor, you can always get the first kid to pick it up.

Pregnancy is nature's way of making sure you're ready to be a mom. After 9 months, you can survive anything.

About the Authors

LINDA PERRET began writing comedy over twenty years ago. She has written for many comedians, including Phyllis Diller, Wendy Liebman, and Terry Fator. Linda was also a staff writer on Bob Hope's 90th Birthday Show on NBC.

She runs an online newsletter for people interested in a career in comedy writing or performing at www.comedywritersroom.com as well as a free joke service for people who want to add a little humor into their lives. This service can be found at www.jokecrafters.com.

In addition to writing comedy, Linda has also worked extensively with Homeowners Associations and authored the book *How to Succeed with Your Homeowners Association.*

GENE PERRET has written comedy since the early 1960s, collecting three Emmys and one Writers Guild award in that time. Gene wrote or produced many of television's iconic shows, including *Laugh-In, The Carol Burnett Show, Three's Company.*

Gene worked with Bob Hope from 1968 until the comic's retirement in the mid-'90s. During that stint, he worked on all of the comic's personal appearances and TV specials and traveled with the Hope troupe to several war zones to work on the legendary comedian's popular Christmas shows.

Perret has also written over forty books on or about humor and several hundred humorous articles for magazines such as *Reader's Digest, McCall's, Arizona Highways,* and others.

As a comedy writing teacher, he has helped launch the careers of several successful writers and comedians.

One of his hobbies is playing the guitar, which has prompted those who hear him play to say, "Thank goodness he went into comedy writing."

About the Artist

ADAM EASTBURN is an up-and-coming artist from California. By day, he is a graphic and motion designer; by night, an illustrator and animator. Adam and his wife, Denise, enjoy travel and James Bond flicks. Find more of his work at adameastburn.net.

About Familius

Welcome to a place where mothers and fathers are celebrated, not belittled. Where values are at the core of happy family life. Where boo-boos are still kissed, cake beaters are still licked, and mistakes are still okay. Welcome to a place where books—and family—are beautiful. Familius: a book publisher dedicated to helping families be happy.

If you feel a few friends and family might benefit from what you've read, let us know and we'll be happy to provide you with quantity discounts. Simply email us at specialorders@familius.com.

Website: www.familius.com
Facebook: www.facebook.com/paterfamilius
Twitter: @familiustalk, @paterfamilius1
Pinterest: www.pinterest.com/familius

The most important work you ever do
will be within the walls of your own home.

FAMILIUS